I could've set back and just let my life pass me bye but no….. I wanted it all not just a little but a lot.

I was willing to do whatever it took to have the luxury of life… that's what my thought said at that time

Not knowing what was in store for me.

I had what a lot of people wanted that's probably why half of these horrible mistaken to be females didn't and was always whispering … huh!

Lisa was you still going to your audition today?

Why? Lisa snapped only because I know this fat ass bitch is just being nosy!

I just asked "mina snapped back.

Lisa was headed to not just to her audition but to meet one of her male friends to handle some business she was falling short with cash a time back last year an inch close to dancing on the stage for the men that visit the classy strip bar off on the strip. On her way to the store a Cadillac truck pulled up towards her she got scared a little but it was broad day light so she wasn't that scared.

Hey sexy a deep voice said to her.

She could tell by the noise of the car it wasn't a bucket so she turned around in a slow but I'm the shit kind of style.

Hey. Lisa called back in her white girl voice

What's your name? He asked

Lisa rolled her eyes and said look I'm sorry but I have to go!

Wait the deep voice called out for her by the time Lisa crossed the street to enter the store the suv was already parked and he was getting out.

Yes! Lisa thought with a smile on her face he went for the old trick.

Lisa was in the store in the produce isle when she heard a phone ring with her favorite song as the ringtone

She looked up and he was standing there looking at her smiling.

What you thought you could get away from me that quick? He said very quickly followed by "look I will make you rich if you're not hard headed!" the man with the deep voice
Stated.

At that moment Lisa was extremely vulnerable so she did something in all of her 24 yrs. of living she have never did… gave an ignorant man some attention hell he did get all the way out of the car which is quite nice by the way… not to mention he got on some clean brand new timberland boot the wheat colored one Lisa very quickly thought of her pros and cons about him so far before she answered.

What make you think you can make me rich? Lisa asked

Because I'm me and you are you the deep voice stated

And who are you? Lisa asked

Uh, sweetheart ladies first. He answered

Listen you are playing games.

Ok ok he said

My name is t.
 Ok my name is l. Lisa said

Chuckles
Why are you laughing Lisa Asked?

Cause I like you already

And every sense then t has been helping Lisa out she do things like just ride with him although she know what he is doing   she never ask and he never tells.

All Lisa does is get real fly and in her priceless shit and they be off in the wind.

Ring, ring, Lisa phone rings as she was walking to her car

Hello?

Where you lady? It was t

Here I come I just left the shop

Man didn't you just get your hair done like 2 days ago chuckles

So what I wanted to get my curls for my audition Lisa said with attitude

When is the audition t asked?

Today. Lisa answered

Lis baby I need you tonight I just got the Cadillac truck washed and I wanted us to head to the concert

What concert Lisa asked?

The Lil Wayne concert.

Before she could answer he was thinking for her or we can go get the Camaro if you want to be low key tonight t tried to bribe Lisa the best way he knew how

Why can't you go with James or Ricky? Lisa asked very quickly before she said yes

They are going t said

Lisa knew they would probably go they were kind of like his rough neck friends that did what t said but with class.

Ok fine but you owe me for missing this audition Lisa stated

Baby fuck that audition you right here with me.

No I'm not t we are not together

Ok I'm just playing but for real whatever you need I got you baby.

Lisa hung the phone up in his ear somewhat pissed and excited for one she knew how important it was to her to go to the audition but being stupid she also longed for a great evening with the fellas.

She could never really bring any of the few lady friends that she did have around.

Lisa tried to bring one of her friends with them but the situation got heavy when her girl started acting like a jealous bitch and made a ghetto ass scene just because the ladies were all over the date that was with her she doesn't know how to chill and at that time I was really on getting money now I'm more laid back I can see clearly.

Besides t thought all my friends are just my friends because of what I got and what I do

He always told me that I was very petty with good hair.

And that broke ass females are going to do me in.... but only if I let them he somewhat teach me shit.

Damn what am I going to wear Lisa thought out loud?

She decided to call her booster that steal whatever she want

Hello

Jamie what's up? Lisa asked into the phone

Shit at the mall

Good I need an outfit for the night

I got the kids with me now I can't bust a move.

Ok Lisa said call me if you can

Ok Jamie said and hung the phone up

The only thing I got was some true jeans with a top brand new but it wasn't classy enough

Ooh wait a light bulb went off in Lisa head she forgot she just got a new dress from babe and it was fly with her Gucci heels and her Gucci bag was ok for the night.

At times Lisa get sad because she misses her family like her sisters and her brother her parents moved to Miami years ago and she decided to stay in old Georgia

She just miss the family thing she was still trying to make it without having to call mom or dad

At that time she wasn't really dating any one sense her and Michael split for fucking her old hair dresser how so consuming she thought when she first found out.

Every sense then her guard has been up.
Lisa tried the whole outfit on and of course with her wearing it was the bomb.

I don't understand how Michael could've cheated on me like this…transforming into my thoughts and attitude thinking how it all came out and he denied it like it was going in style.

I look so good in this dress I want to fuck myself tonight

Ring Lisa phone rung

Hello

A Lisa I need you to get dress like in the next hour

What? Lisa asked

Man lies baby u heard me I'm not into this shit right now so get dressed I want to go eat before the concert

Lisa knew that smart talking meant business, t always had a nice swag to him but when he get upset she knew that he meant what he said

Shit this man is the man around here and everybody listened except me. Until now

Ok Lisa answered

T Lisa called his name before the phone hung up

Yea t answered

Where we going to eat at?

Where ever you want to go but I'm staving like Marvin

His corny ass jokes alright Lisa hung the phone up

Lisa sat there for a while wondering about her audition and how it would've went if she did go

The next best actress of the year goes to Lisa Sanchez. The crowd clapped so loud all you could hear was people screaming Lisa walked on the stage with her whole family even her little niece was on stage with the whole family
I want to thank every person that really been there, my parents Lisa turned to her mother and with a smile she turned back to her audience that was making her feel on top of her game suddenly

Ring

You ready? It was t calling

Yes? Lisa answered telling a fib she had just woken up from a very important dream but she couldn't remember all of it in detail

Stop it. T new when Lisa was lying

No really aim! Lisa argued with a serious voice

Well come on then I'm about to be pulling up in about 20 mines
0 my goodness Lisa thought I only have 20 minutes to wash my ass. This is crazy but I think I can manage. Bye she hung the phone up ran to her room and grabbed one of her victories secrets set out from her clothing closet and went into the bathroom where she so did not keep her bathing towels so very quickly she went back to the hallway where she kept her

bathing towels in a hallway closet turned back around entering the bathroom

One thing Lisa had had over people was the fact that she prayed a lot of people around her did not so much believe in the spiritual blessings so before she left the house at times was the times she would pray

So very quickly while letting the water get hot she said a little prayer very

Lord bless us as we got to and from home I love u bye!

She went to church with her family all of the time before they moved and silly old Lisa stayed because of Michael who turned out to be a joke

Damn! Lisa screamed the hot water was super-hot before she knew it

The water felt so good in washing my body very quickly I couldn't just take a hoe bath

Lisa thought my body need to smelling super good besides the restaurant isn't going anywhere Lisa thought

Getting out of the shower going straight to the bedroom drying off while walking towards the bathroom thinking about how Michael used to wait until she got out of the shower to surprise her with a beautiful feeling of his tongue on her body all over her body

Taking the tags off of the entire set took way longer than the shower shit Lisa groaned

Finally putting her dress that she had just took off from trying on back on

She didn't really think that she would need a coat so took a lace throw that went perfect with what she was wearing

Putting her make up on the phone rung

Hello! Lisa answered already knowing it was t

I'm outside

Ok here I come Lisa said

Lisa ran to grab her Gucci bag that was in the closet with the rest of her bags

Switched her wallet to her Gucci bag then grabbing her mac powder just in case she needed a cleanup while out with her viva glam lip glaze

Turning back towards her bedroom to grab her Gucci glasses she changed her mind maybe that will be too much she thought I can just wear my plain school girl glasses

Getting her keys she grabbed a few hundred bills from her stash in the kitchen in which she been meaning to switch spots after she accidently gave a tip to the delivery guy last

week who watched her grab the 2o dollar bill from the box in her cabinet
Lisa know that she don' t need a penny while she is with t but with the attitude Lisa have

She tried to always stay on her toes

Out the door locking it from the corner of Lisa eye she see a shadow walking up so looked all the way up and it was her maintenance guy going into her neighbor's apartment

Walking out the building not knowing which car t is driving she looked to see surprisingly he was driving the Cadillac truck

Lisa got in the truck we got to go switch cars real quick t rushed and said with a smile on his face like I already know what you about to say.

T I don't feel like this shit I got my Gucci heels on Lisa whined

So u want to stay in this? T asked

I don't care because I don't want to move until we get where we going

Alright t answered

They headed to express way when t asked what you want to eat.

I want some shrimp and steak with sushi she answered with her mind already made up

Look the concert uptown from here it should take us about 30 mins to get there from here t said stern

But that was just how it was very stern and loveable at times Lisa thought it was serious when he was always playing

T pulled up in this restaurant that was so beautiful, and people was greeting us at the front door to park the car for us

We entered this restaurant that had water pouring when you first go in

Bye time we were seated it was women walking around in barely anything

T what type of place is this Lisa asked pissd off

Baby it's a restaurant that got good food he laughed while looking at the menu

Lisa rolled her eyes forget it she thought

Hi I will be your waitress this yellow girl stood beside the table are you ready to order?

Can I have a bottle of Moet? T asked right off the back nothing new Lisa thought

And can I have the steak, shrimp and sushi platter Lisa spoke to the waitress while looking in her bag for the phone which was ringing effusively poor Lisa couldn't find it because she was carrying a big bag that had stuff in it every sense the last time she wore it to the last runway show that was here in November

By time Lisa found her phone it had stopped ringing

And you sir? The waitress asked t

I will have the shrimp platter with the scampies

Where is the boys? Lisa asked

They coming they have to handle something first t answered you look nice little girl t said in his deep usual voice

I hate when t called me little girl

I am not a little girl Lisa said while checking her phone for missed calls

One of her friends from school was calling she had been friends with holly for a long time but when holly got pregnant she changed and went back to   being a jealous bitch like the rest of the females that used   to start shit with Lisa

Back in the day Lisa was always into it with a female the reason being still trying to figure it out!

I will call her back later she probably don't want shit

After eating all that food Lisa and t left the restaurant and on their way out Lisa noticed t stopped and looked at this man   as if he seen a ghost

Come here Lisa

What? Lisa asked

Did you hear me t asked in a deep voice even deeper than usual but not too loud

Lisa went back a little towards t to see why he was looking and acting a little crazy

What's the matter with you t?

Lisa asked with suspension

T grabbed Lisa arm very soft but tight and said just hold on a moment baby

Lisa noticed how sweaty t's hand was which was very unusual

After standing there with t Lisa felt irritated after watching the lady and her man friend looking at her and t as if they were about to rob the place

T eventually started walking out Lisa went along with the action and as she walked out she noticed 2 men standing at the bar part of the amazing restaurant he looked scary to her by time she got to the door she looked back at the 2 men and noticed that one of them turned towards her and watched t walk to the truck the valet was handing t the keys

Lisa followed and got into the car before she could ask any questions t had the music turned off

Lis baby I got something I need to keep at your house for a few days

Umm ok I guess Lisa responded in a soft voice

Pulling up to the place where the concert was at the line was so long Lisa didn't want to say it but she hoped that t knew she wasn't hardly standing in a line

She just kept quiet knowing now was not the time to be starting arguments with t instead she just sat back for the night with so many thoughts in her head

Walking up to the door Lisa looking like a million dollar gal she could feel the stares but didn't pay attention Lisa attitude is she not into giving anyone any chances at this time it's getting money that's in her brain

T got to the front door asking for VIP by time Lisa got all the way to the door t was waiting for her so they could go in

Inside of the place it was so many people there we went straight to VIP where it was nothing but females so Lisa did the ultimate and told t she was going to Mingo in the other crowd

T hated when she did that he thought she was a little girl for real

No stay in here t snapped

What is his problem Lisa wondered?

A lady walked up to the table they was sitting at and offered a bottle of Moet

Yes can I have two of them t asked

The lady left and came back with two bottles of Moet not knowing her skirt was up in the back t told her and made her laugh clearly she thought he was cute in which t is handsome so it's to be expected

I popped my bottle not waiting on t I hear the song Lil Wayne going on stage

I want to go to the front Lisa complained

Ok go ahead but get back here in a minute I'm cool right here I'm waiting on the boys to get here

Ok Lisa said

Walking towards the stage Lisa seen one guy from Lil Wayne's entourage eyeballing her so Lisa decided to look back at him she continued til she got to the stage

Lil Wayne performed a few more songs before they got off the stage as the entourage walked off stage the guy asked her Lisa to come with them it only was Wayne and another female not thinking Lisa went continuing to walk through with the rest of the people the they were with 1..
 Was stopped by the security guard Lisa laughed by that time she was feeling the Moet in her system she didn't even care but the guy turned around and told the security guy that Lisa was with them

At that time Lisa was feeling worthy of herself continuing to walk down some steps entering a room before you knew it Lisa was standing there in the room with the guy who was eyeballing her and ill Wayne with the young lady he was with while him and Lil Wayne rush to the snacks on the table me and the other young lady stood there of course she looked at Lisa as if she wanted to say bitch Lisa waiting to curse her if needed shit she the one with Wayne.

A knock on the door made everyone quiet Wayne answered it it was a man telling I'm that his ride was outside the guy that was staring asked Lisa "are you ready"? Lisa wondering ready for what
Answered yes I'm ready

Lil Wayne and the young lady walked out and Lisa and the guy staring walked behind them. All of a sudden all you heard was Wayne... Wayne I love you he stopped so we all stopped to take a few pictures that some people wanted to take before we left out the door.

Walking out the door there was a stretched navigator limo waiting while waiting to get in the limo Lisa could hear a familiar voice screaming "a groupie. A groupie" Lisa looked up to see t standing there across the street watching Lisa.

Lisa stood there not knowing what to do the guy that was staring looked at Lisa while entering the limo Lisa just looked him in eyes and then turned around to go back through the door

Damn Lisa thought who knows what could've came out of that

On her back outside towards t who was waiting for her at the door

Super star he greeted her with a big smile

How u gone just leave me for them? He asked laughing so hard

I just wanted to see how far I could go Lisa stated in embarrassment

Go where to get fucked! T said still with his little laugh that was irking Lisa nerves

Whatever Lisa didn't argue

Finally in the car tired from a long night Lisa was finally up to asking t about earlier that day at the restaurant

But then again. She changed her mind hell... she thought he will tell me when he ready

Pulling up to Lisa house t turned the car off and there was an awkward silence

Lisa here he handed her a little bag Lisa didn't ask no questions she just put it in her Gucci bag

Alright t I will call u in the morning Lisa said while getting out of the car

Alright I need you to roll to the city with me in the morning so please be ready man
I will be here at 7am sharp lady t said with a serious look

O hold on t reached in his pocket and handed Lisa a ball of money she noticed the hundred dollar bill on top

Lisa reached for it thank you Lisa said with a concern attitude unbelievably his hands were still sweaty like they were earlier that day

Why are your hands so sweaty like wet t? Lisa asked in concern

Umm I don't know they just always sweaty baby t answered

Ok mar tony Lisa said with kind of smirk on her face as if she knew different

That's ok... Lisa thought I will talk to him a little more in the morning this isn't regular for him to be acting this away.

By time I got to my apartment I was exhausted from everything including the fact that I missed one of the most important auditions ever but never mind that I'm sure there will be more I have to see what is in this bag.

Then she thought never mind I will be loyal like he want me to be but he didn't tell Lisa not too but instead she put the bag away in her panty drawer first but then changed her mind that's a stupid idea she thought that's where a robber would go first if was to enter a lady's room

So perhaps under her bed would be better after letting her mattress fall she went to get a quick shower and before she could count to 100 she was out like light

Lisa ....Lisa...wake up girl lets go to breakfast...

Lisa opened her eyes to see that it was her mother in front of her with a nice hair do that looked a little than normal but it was nice it said I'm back in my twenties

Mom where you want to go?

Lisa I thought you wanted me to try that new Mr. Chow restaurant in Vegas Mrs. Lainey answered

Mr. Chow.........Lisa thought but that's way in Vegas and how was we getting there mom? Lisa asked

Lisa we already got our tickets your secretary said there waiting for us at the airport in gate 8

My secretary... Lisa looked around at where she was laying at and it looked unfamiliar

But flawless like lists kind of taste with the leather and suede furniture with 2 big flat screens in the living area and one in the kitchen area and she could see everything from where she was laying at. Lisa got up rushing to see the rest of the house headed straight to her bedroom where ever that was

rushing passed the kitchen taking a quick glance but stopped and stand by the kitchen flooring it was so beautiful It looked like glass flooring Lisa type of party she continued to walk towards her room when she noticed a jumbo sized picture of herself with silk gloves and beautiful diamond bracelets on both wrist and a ultimately happy smile her make was extremely flawless with the Marilyn Monroe pin up hairstyle not just any hairstyle but a rich fancy white girl style in the biggest frame she had ever seen

Ring ring ring ring

With slobber foaming on her mouth Lisa reached over to grab her phone to hear t voice

You ready sweetheart?

Sometimes it felt as if t thought that Lisa was his girl at one point in time to beat this boy so bad just for complimenting her I guess it was because this guy was drunk and he touched her ass that really mad Lisa pissed if she wasn't drunk she probably wouldn't been laughing that hard after he did it .that night was horror she begged t to stop it wasn't cute what t did I figured the man was a little loose and he simply didn't mean it unfortunately t didn't agree at all instead he made him apologize to her and every time he happen to see her
I'm almost ready Lisa answered lying to t and herself

Ok I'm pulling up are you hungry?

Umm not really

Ok

Here I come Lisa rushed and hung the phone up

Reaching for her robe she got up and headed to bathroom feeling delightful after a dream but not remembering hardly any of it except her picture she kept thinking of. Rushing brushing her teeth and washing her body at the same time was very filthy to Lisa but she had to hurry and get down stairs

Finally prepared to go downstairs running to her spot to grab some cash she forgot that t had just handed her some in her hand last night if I could just remember where I put it

Grabbing her Gucci bag from the night before she found the roll on top of her bag

Willing to count it before she go out the door.

Damn this is cool Lisa thought …counting fifteen hundred dollars she kept five and put the rest up

Going out of the door looked to make sure all of her lights were out except the one in the kitchen

T was out of the car doing something in the trunk then all of a sudden Lisa   hear the music getting louder and louder than boom boom   the sound of that new this was blazing

Baby you ready? T asked

Lisa shook her head yes all cute happy to see t rolling the new Camaro

I mean why don't he drive it shit it's our if he thought Lisa smiled I mean his

Besides Lisa was rolling a new Monte Carlos been driving it before it even hit the area

She figure it was time to switch up it's been almost 3 yrs.

Getting in the car t asked Lisa what she wanted to hear "umm it doesn't matter what u got? Lisa asked"

T phone started ringing "hello"

What's up t started talking on the phone? "What's up man" it seemed as if it was getting a little aggressive with his voice

Not knowing what was going on Lisa continued to try to finish putting her mascara on

T man hang the phone up you not driving right Lisa stated a little loud enough so it could hear her

T hung the phone up

Lis baby I'm going to take u back to the crib very quickly I have to handle something

Why can't I just ride if you're coming right back Lisa asked in a confused voice

T just looked at her and said baby I will be right back just be ready girl now you got time to put your make up on like you was going to one of your auditions or something

Whatever Lisa said while rolling her eyes

You better hurry up Lisa told t

AL rite he said with a smile that looked so pure

Regarding the fact that she was interrupted from not only her sleep but her dream that seemed so nice but unable to reconcile exactly what it was about

Lisa walked up to her apartment just in time to watch the Tyra banks show and the episode about super head was on

I just don't understand what Tyra's motive was to bring karrine Stefan's on the show if she was blatantly   going humiliate her I mean damn she is spilling herself out to you and all you can seem to do is bring up negative things

Wait everything she was doing was negative Lisa reevaluated her attitude

But still why humiliate her clearly she was being what she wanted to be which was a slut

But hell my mind frame is the same way "fuck a nigga like rick Ross said "money make me cum" o my goodness and he aunt never lied just thinking about it is making my pussy tingle clean everything

Getting overly exhausted Lisa sat on the couch it was now 11:00

And t still hadn't called her

Lisa decided to call t's phone it just kept picking up on the first ring

You have reached the sprint pcs voice mailbox please leave a message..beeeeeeeep

Oooh Lisa kept getting irritated

Forget it Lisa thought maybe he busy.

Lisa decided to go for a ride to the nail salon just to change the color of her nails

Listening to Trina

Before she could get into the song her phone was ringing

Hello?

Lisa hear nothing but screaming in the background

"Those mouthafuckas got me fucked up "

The voice sounded familiar

Hello who the fuck is this? Lisa asked sounding like she as upset already she knew something was wrong

"Lisa they got em man they got him Lisa "l

Lisa finally knew who the voice was

Ricky what are u talking about dude? Lisa getting even more upset

Man tonoi is dead man Ricky said crying like he had just lost his best friend in which he did He called t by his government name

Lisa felt chills all through her body she stopped the car and just stayed in drive Ricky please Lisa begging Ricky for what she didn't know she couldn't hardly speak

Rick baby please tell me what happened

But she couldn't listen where the hell u at? Lisa wanted to know where he was to look him in the face

Her main man was gone so he say but she needed to be there

Where the fuck he at? Lisa asked pissed not really functioning t was gone

Lisa baby they got him at the hospital don't go you don't need

Before Ricky could finish speaking Lisa hung the phone up now going 60 down the street

Not knowing which hospital he was at she had two to choose from she went to the first one closest so mad she couldn't call Ricky she didn't know what happened he could be the enemy

Pulling up to the memorial hospital she noticed an older lady crying in the entrance and people all over Lisa stopped the car and ran straight to the desk please where Antonio Walters's room is? The lady already obviously new because by time she finished asking she already had the paper written out Looking sad as if she knew him too.

Lisa ran to room 305 as fast as possible not really even catching her breathe before you knew it she was getting off the elevator on the third floor she just followed the screams

Before Lisa got to the room she fell to her knees crying

Please Jesus please Jesus please Lisa cried

Trina came over to Lisa

Lisa its ok Trina rubbed Lisa's back

Trina was a friend of tonios she had been dealing with him for years

Lisa sat there for a few minutes she finally got up and slowly walked to the room and and finally looking at t

His lifeless body just lying there with his eyes still opened as if he wanted to say something Lisa walked towards him barely able to see because of her eyes and lashes soaked with tears her nose running she was sick at this point of time in her life

She touched his hand and rubbed it back and forth feeling nothing but coldness

She stood there thinking about the time when he told her "life is short and you have to trust somebody"

Lisa opened up her eyes and wipe her face stood there for about 25 more minutes it felt as if it was only her and t in the room but she knew it was other people in there as well

A person came in the room she didn't know who it was because she couldn't turn around she was still in shock a little

She heard a voice we will now be moving the body now

It was a women's voice Lisa could hear the footsteps of people leaving

Lisa grabbed her black coach sunglasses and rubbed t's hand one more time and walked out of the room

On her way down the hallway she heard someone calling her name

Lisa turned around to see it was tonio's little brother

She tried to sniffle up real fast she wanted to be able to accommodate that he was hurt and needed a shoulder as well too

She stood there till he reached her

Man this shit is crazy lil babe said to her

What happened babe? Lisa asked

We was in the car and he kept saying that "we got to hurry up these niggas tripping!"

What niggas Lisa asked

They not from here and I haven't ever seen these jokers lil babe answered

We was just sitting at the stop sign when his phone rung he answered it then all of a sudden a car pulls up and then a girl get out of the car and just start busting all over the place so I ducked and didn't think to look at tonio by time the guns stopped the car had gurperd off real fast

Lisa stood there in disbelief shaking her head thinking about what he had just said

So you said a female Lisa asked
Yes mamma lil babe responded in assurance that it was a female

What she look like Lisa asked

A dead bitch lil babe answered

Lisa turned around and just left the hospital completely

After hearing and taking in the fact that a bitch killed my friend, my homie for life

She almost couldn't breathe her pussy got wet thinking about killing this bitch

Who is she Lisa thought out loud

Lisa phone rung

Hello Lisa answered

Baby are you ok? It was Lisa's mother

Mom mom they killed my friend Lisa started hollering while driving feeling the tears getting a little splash into her eyes

I know baby it will be ok just calm down Lisa's mother tried to calm her down

It hurt mom my only friend that was here for me Lisa stated crying even more hard

It will be ok baby why don't you try to get a flight to come here ok

No how would I be able to do that mom my friend just got murdered Lisa argued as if she could beat the world

"Listen to me" Mrs. Elaine voice got very strange as if she had blood on her hands

You don't go do nothing crazy girl I can't take it and hung the phone up

At that moment Lisa knew her mother was not into the bullshit but what she didn't understand was the fact that at that time Lisa was on one

She decided to call   and get some marijuana   from a friend that been having it for a while Lisa don't really smoke but right now at that moment it was a must and he had that good Kush that she smoked nothing less she thought if I'm gone insert smoke in the body hell it should be the best

After the little ounce of Kush from her friend she decided to just go home get high and call her mother back and apologize to the one person in the whole world that she knew gave a fuck about her

Heading to her apartment she seen a few people standing outside

She still just parked her car as usual

Lisa got out of the car and went headed for her apartment

Lisa went straight to the kitchen to roll her blunt

Shortly finishing up her phone rung

Hello Lisa answered

It was James. What's up with it?

At home chilling man this shit is crazy Lisa took a deep breathe

I know James answered   I just spoke with lil babe and he said it was a bitch that did that shit like he said somebody told him she was from here but her peoples was the ones from out of town on some bullshit. Check t was saying that he had just met another connect from this girl that he knew

O yeah Lisa asked

She from them little projects on the sizzle James said

Lisa agreed to meet up with James and Ricky later to have a few drinks

Lisa inhaled and exhaled a few times and felt on top of the world

After getting extremely high Lisa went into her bedroom to get her silk rob

Thinking about who this rat bitch is that killed her friend

Falling asleep was no option at this time she managed to stay up

Remembering t told Lisa to hold something for him

Immediately Lisa went to it unwrapped it

Omg....Lisa stood there with her mouth wide open

What am I supposed to do with this? Lisa thought out loud

The shiny tiny little diamonds just sitting there looking like they ready..

Lisa hurried and went to her door to make sure all locks were on

Lisa was so high that she was paranoid then she went to the windows of her apartment checking every last one of them

Ok.. She thought

Lisa went back to the diamonds and counted them

It was 50 small diamonds

Damn Lisa thought what if this is the reason behind t death

Lisa thoughts were starting to get to her
I got to think outside the box not knowing rather to keep this to herself or follow-up on the mission

Furthermore Lisa didn't even know what the mission was however she knew she had these diamonds

Lisa decided to just chill and think more into the situation she had to meet up with the boys in a hot second

"Should I tell them or just see what they tell me "Lisa thought

Wishing that t was there to help her figure this out but then again situated wouldn't have occurred

Knock…knock…

Lisa eyes got so scared someone was knocking at her door

Lisa quickly wiped her tears put the diamonds up and went to the peep hole

Who is it? Lisa asked

Lil babe the deep voice said real quickly

Lisa opened the door

Wants up babe? Lisa said

I'm sorry sorry for popping up on you but you know these phones crazy lil babe stated

Lisa thought here we go with these phones and shit Lisa didn't know rather to believe that or not it seem like everybody thought that though so she just always took it into consideration

It cool what's up? Lisa answered

I know that you and t was close as fuck so I figured I would tell you that I knew he was doing some other type of shit on the other side and I knew he was meeting up with these rich as people I mean baby I know we rolling in something but these niggas was like white boy rich with diamonds and shit..Lisa almost choked after lil babe said that

You ok lil babe asked

Yes I'm fine Lisa lied wondering if now was the time to tell lil babe but if t had the diamonds then what was the issue? Lisa thought

So I don't know what happened to the transaction but in the mean time I think that was a major set up I got white boys number him and the Mexicans number t had hollered at me last week about some shit lil babe said

I don't know if Ricky and James know anything bout this so till we figure some shit out hold on telling them any thing
Lil babe was specific

I guess I will meet with them in a second Lisa responded

Call them niggas and see where they at now lil babe said sounding like t….. The only thing was that he wasn't t

Hold on let me think real quick Lisa said

She walked towards her room wanting to show lil babe the diamonds but something wouldn't let her

Ok I'm about to call

Hello James picked up on the first ring

What's up Lisa asked

Where you at James asked

At home Lisa answered

You ready James asked

Ready for what Lisa asked

To link up he answered

Yea just come by I'm not in the mood to leave the house I might hurt somebody Lisa said to James

Ok give me a minute I'm on my way

What he say lil babe asked the minute Lisa took the phone from her hear

He said he will be here in a minute

Ok

Man this shit is so crazy lil babe just sat on the ottoman not knowing how uncomfortable he looked just like he lost his big brother somewhat still in shock in which I knew he was because I was to

All of a sudden Lisa heard warm crying coming from where he was sitting

Lisa decided to get up and just go to her room for a second at this point a time in her life she couldn't help this young man at this point of time in her life her heart was burning too

Lisa wanted to call her family but she didn't instead she just sat in shock and partially disbelief

Shortly after staring In space Lisa heard the noise of rick's car pull up so she got up and went to the front room and seen that lil babe was still in his mood of shock until the knock on the door

Knowing who it was Lisa asked "who is it?"

It's me James answered in a low voice

Lisa opened the door and walked away

What's up Ricky asked walking in behind James

Nobody said nothing but he knew everybody was there and ready to discuss

Although Lisa was a high class polished lady she still had her rough attitude behind her like a weapon so she was prepared for whatever she needed to be focus not knowing what could be next

I mean do any of u knew these new people t was dealing with James asked

Lisa was silent and so was everyone else

Lil babe what's up u didn't know shit James went straight to the next person he knew had information

No not really lil babe answered

Lisa couldn't believe her ears or understand but it had to be a reason as to why he want it a secret so she kept quiet

We just need to watch our back Ricky suggested

Still silent lil babe got up from the ottoman after a few hours of just sitting there

He walked to the door and stood for a second

I'm about to go Lisa call me later then turned to Ricky and James and said get at me about this funeral bullshit man

Before he could finish James said man that's been taken care of just let me know when u can get fitted for your shit

What shit lil babe asked

Your tucks we taken him home in style just how my nigga like it you heard James asked

Lil babe walked out the door

Still sitting there Lisa decided to roll another blunt hell go hard or go home she thought with a tear rolling down her face

I just can't believe it Lisa blurted out

Me neither but the shit don't add up why and who would do this we don't owe or got beef right now Ricky said

That's what I was thinking Lisa agreed

Smoking and thinking is all Lisa did when James and Ricky left

The next day Lisa got up off her Couche in which she slept on all night for the first time ever

Looked around her to make sure she wasn't dreaming still in disbelief

She got in the shower and decided to go to the library and look up the values of real diamonds then possibly go get them priced but not just yet it was too hot

When Lisa arrived at the library she noticed it was packed every sense her computer got a virus she hasn't had time to get it fixed although she was in desperate need to get it fixed instead of coming to this public library

Lisa decided to go back home she wasn't feeling the outside at this time but wanted to order some food to go from her and t's favorite spot a little restaurant called papadeaux they had some great shrimp and steak that they loved

Sitting at the bar waiting for her to go order a man came in to   the door and sat right next to Lisa

It made her very uncomfortable but he smelled clean it didn't matter Lisa wasn't in the mood for no judging shit she had lost a great friend

Would you like another drink the waiter asked Lisa?

Yes please Lisa responded without looking up at the lady who was serving her

Excuse me miss the soft voice interrupted Lisa's thinking

Lisa turned towards the voice to make sure the person was speaking to her

After eye contact Lisa still decided to ignore this guy she just felt terrible and was not at her best at this time

After a few minutes the soft voice guy got up and walked out of the restaurant no noticing the fact that he had just paid for Lisa's bill

Can I have my bill please Lisa asked the waitress as she discreetly walked passed her

The waiter stopped and looked around s if she was looking for someone

O I'm sorry the waitress responded the gentlemen that was here next to you just paid for your bill

Still in disbelief the waiter looked around one last time before she asked

Is there anything else I can get for you?

By that time Lisa was putting her sunglasses back on and was out the door

Walking to the side walk Lisa could feel something or someone watching her she decided to just stop and look around herself

I'm not on no bullshit it's you want to take me out as well then whatever Lisa thought

Still in paranoia Lisa decided to hold still and get on her cellphone and pose as if she was making or answering a call

A car was moving behind her she decided to turn around it was a black suv

She kept turning until the direction she was going she spotted a pink beamer that went flying up the

Street instead of paying attention to the suv she was just on another though at that time

Beep beep omg before Lisa new it she was in the middle of the street with a car beeping at her to turn

Right.

Lisa hurried across the street to her car and pressing the unlock button when the same suv pulled up

Excuse me pretty lady the voice was so deep that Lisa decided to ignore him

Finally the door open and Lisa getting into the car and turning the key I need to get home is all Lisa

Thought so paranoid…

Maam are you ok?

Omg the same voice from the restaurant was at her car door

I'm fine Lisa said as she looked up to this big handsome gentleman that smelled like baby lotion

Lisa smiled to think of him smelling the same way t smelled he used nothing but baby lotion with a little fragrance cologne at times

Ok umm I was wondering r u married? The guy with the same voice not knowing if It was him or not

No aim not married and I'm running late for something I have to go thank you Lisa said very quickly before starting her car to let the handsome guy know that she was very serious

What I look like I just lost my close friend to me

Fuck any and everything besides figuring some things out besides I'm not in the dating mood

Lisa slammed the door and pulled off checking on her surroundings before ultimately pulling down the

Street.

Turning her Monica on to her favorite song playing on the cd she bumped all the way home

In tears before she made it home Lisa decided to turn the music off and just think finally not high or to buzz

Who the fuck did this to my friend balling barely able to see the road Lisa finally at the parking entrance to her home

She turned the car off and just sat there in silence no noise not even neighbors outside or nothing just silence

Wait if a female shot t then who is the people from out of town and why would she want to do this

Lisa wanted to think outside of the box

If I was to kill a man why would I ….

Lisa couldn't really come up with no reasons   intentionally to kill anyone no matter how hard her crew was they wanted do nothing unless need be at all times getting money was the motive

That's what got me puzzled Lisa thought before deciding to get out of the car and going to her apartment

After walking to her door she noticed a shadow Lisa quickly turned around to get clearer view

It was her little old lady neighbor that from time to time bring her over fruit pies that Lisa absolutely did not like

Hi leez baby is what she called her

Hi Mr.'s Luna how are you? Lisa asked

I'm fine how are you mars Luna asked before Lisa could answer mars Luna was grabbing her as if she knew exactly what Lisa needed

Lisa fell to her knees she had never been through something like this in her life

Mrs. Luna whispered in her ear "it will be alright child"

Lisa got up off the clean hallway floors and sniffled a little unable to smile still

I will see you later Lisa responded and entered her apartment and closed the door

Without Mrs. Luna even speaking of it she knew

Mrs. Luna has been Lisa's neighbor for a while now and she may not speak much but she know much

Lisa went straight to the diamond stash to make sure still this is real

So paranoid still Lisa grabbed the stash checked to make sure all of them was there right then Lisa knew

She shouldn't smoke anymore that shit right there would have her messed up in the situation that she was in

Lisa figured she need to stay focused at all times not knowing what the next move was

Ring ring ring Lisa looked at the caller id it was him the nigga that ruined her attitude towards certain men at times she decided not to answer

Lisa kicked her shoes off and ate her food from the little place and all of a sudden

Lisa wake up Lisa woke up and could see a room full of flowers and her sister standing over her

Lisa come on you to get on stage now

I can't Nicole I can't Lisa argued

But you have to remember they just paid you 15,000 just to be present

Lisa looked behind her and seen that her father was sitting there as if he was in disbelief

Nicole she is heartbroken let her be

Its ok Lisa said as she stood in a one piece red sequence down suit it was beautiful

Walking into the restroom looking at herself Lisa thought she seen a ghost

Ring ring ring ring

Hello not knowing who it was Lisa answered before looking at the caller id

Hey Lisa   a small but loud voice

Still have sleep Lisa answered again this time a little more firm hello

It was no answer
Lisa hung the phone up

I may as well get up and go get in the shower and eat the rest of my food

Not knowing the evening was going to be like Lisa decided to put on a little more casual outfit not too much or too little
Almost falling into another little sleep nap Lisa almost forgot her water was running

After getting dressed in her little be be t-shirt and be be jeans she sat down in the kitchen looking at her floor thinking where do I start damn

She decided to go ahead to get some car books to look for another car

Lisa was definitely determined to play her cards right to figure out what happened and keep the money flowing

Forget it Lisa thought I'm going to have to turn lil babe on to what's the deal but first I need to make sure what the prices on the diamonds are before he knows anything just in case he try any funny shit but Lisa figure hell it wasn't hers from the get so why not share the wealth with her own people

Lisa wanted to also to get situated for the funeral but what if she did the unthinkable and didn't go understanding the fact that the whole city knew how close the two of them were why not stay low key

Lisa couldn't believe her attitude but it was what it was a dog ass bitch for the time being

Heading out to her car Lisa noticed some crazy smell outside as if something was on fire but shit she kept walking hell it aunt my place to say shit to no one but this young lady

Keeping her thoughts and mouth close until then

The lady at the register at the little store that Lisa went to to grab a simple car book

My car is what u can always catch me in but not if I switch it up till later

Lisa thought

Wondering just how slick these people could be Lisa wanted to go ahead and head back home to call lil babe

One mind is great to have BUT TWO MINDS ARE MAGNIFICENT

It was kind of scary to Lisa but the feel of her lost one was even scarier Lisa and t had plans together

And whoever this mystery chick bitch is need to know just that

By the end of the day Lisa had accomplished

A whole lot of things

She had a short conversation with the jeweler and he arranged for his management to give her a call

Lisa had not sat down and talked to lil babe yet waiting on the jeweler to let her know how much exactly Lisa was working with

I guess I can go to a little exercising just to kill a little time

Pulling up to body fitness Lisa noticed a few people standing outside of the gym it looked like they were having a cigarette break maybe

Grabbing her lil pepper spray seeing that's all she could take in the building with her if that she opened the door after parking her car in a handicap space thanks to Lisa's friend that let her buy it from her

Grabbing her gym bag and shutting the door Lisa walked up to the main entrance noticing a young lady standing there looking at Lisa as if she knew her with a little smirk on her face

Ignoring the lil female Lisa entered the door straight to the front desk

Before Lisa got to the desk the lady starring outside was at the desk

Hi welcome to body fitness the starring lady said

Hi Lisa repeated I would like to work out today and I don't have a membership

Ok...would you like to purchase a membership today ma'am? Starring lady asked

Not at this time I would like to just workout Lisa answered

Ring ring ring

Lisa looked at her phone it was lil babe

Not answering the phone Lisa signed the paper and grabbed her bag and went to the gym

I have to wait till I talk to lil babe I'm still waiting on the jeweler Lisa thought

Inside the gym it was a few other people inside the gym room''

Lisa went straight to the weights

I definitely want to get my strength up before any action Lisa laughed a little to herself

Thinking about how T used to make fun of him calling her a little girl

Thinking about T made Lisa just sit there in thought for few seconds until a hand touched Lisa shoulder

Excuse me ma'am re u going to use these weights? The voice of a male asked

I sure am Lisa answered

The man walked away looking around as if he was still looking for the weights that I have

Starting to count to myself as I lifted the first weight

Not knowing rather I should do sit ups or crunches Lisa had benched 100 with the weights

She decided to just do crunches at least 65

Lisa finally finished and went to the shower room
'
Feeling uncomfortable taking a shower somewhere other than home was kind of awkward for Lisa

Drying off her body and putting on some thongs that Lisa had just got from Victoria's secret and a nice little sweat suit as well

Lisa worked up an appetite deciding to grab something to eat again Lisa headed home

Ring ring ring ring

Grabbing the phone from the bottom of her gym bag Lisa had already missed the call

Looking at the caller I'd it was the jeweler

Redialing the number the phone on the other end was ringing

Thank you for calling Tim pond shop this is Tim how may I help u

Hi I just got a call from you this is Lisa Lisa answered

O hello maam I got some information for you I got with mu management and the prices for those type of diamonds are very exclusive and I would love to make an offer

 DaMN Lisa thought he got straight to the point

Kind of wanting a second opinion Lisa just continued to listen

The value of them are 250.000 thousand dollars and what we want to offer 220.000 thousand he finally was finished

Would that be cash? Lisa asked

It can be cash the Tim gut said

Ok I want to consult a few things and would like at least 24 hours to consider with the option of you not telling anyone ever about this transaction? Lisa asked

The phone was silent

Hello Lisa said

Yes I'm here the Tim gut answered

I want to but what about I getting rid of them how am I suppose to make profit the Tim guy continued

Not evening knowing where they come from

Lisa not in the mood starting to think about T and I how if he was here he would've took care of this shit

Again Mr. Tim I will need 24 hours and clearly you do too so how about we get together in the am Lisa asked

That's sounds good mar Tim answered

Hanging the phone up and getting out of the car and heading to her house Lisa heard someone talking maybe trying to   talk to her but Lisa kept walking she didn't feel up to talking

Lisa Lisa the voice was getting closer Lisa turned around and seen who appeared to be omg….

Michael Lisa called out

Hey how are you doing Michael Answered?

Lisa standing there in disturbance like what does he want Lisa Thought?

I wanted to come check on you Lisa Michael said

Mike I mean Michael Lisa caught herself before giving Michael the pleasure if Lisa calling him her little pet name when they were together

You could've called me Lisa continued very quickly

I wanted to see you baby Michael answered

 I'm not your baby Lisa said in a manner that Michael knew she was serious

Come here Michael told Lisa

What Lisa asked

Come here Michael repeated

Lisa slowly walked towards him and he walked towards her he just extended one of his arms to her while the other rubbed through her hair leaning forward to smell it just how he used to….that's enough Lisa stopped him

Don't act like that Lisa it's been so long baby! Michael said in a polite slow and soft voice

Lisa decided to just walk up the steps to her building and shut the door leaving Michael standing there now Lisa did not feel in the mood for apologies   he can save them for the next young lady he walk all over besides he probably just wanted her reaction and it was just that

Ring ring ring looking at the caller id she seen it was Ricky but she didn't answer

Thinking that she left her cabinets open Lisa continued to walk to her bedroom

Ayyyyyyy Lisa screamed to the top of her longs inside Lisa bedroom was a dead rat laying on her bed with clothes and bags a jewelry all over the place running to the front door someone grabbed her hair and pulled her down to the ground while putting a knife to her neck

Move I will slice u bitch said an unfamiliar lady voice

Who are u Lisa asked loudly

Lisa all of a sudden felt a slap to her left cheek leaving Lisa applaud

Lisa quickly turned the lady with her arm that the knife was in
While quickly turning around and grabbing whatever it was on the lady body that seemed to be her neck
while holding on to the arm with the knife in it the lady must've knew karate because by time Lisa had her
neck she was falling to the ground again before she could see anything she seen the all black dressed lady
fleeing out her front door

Damn Lisa thought I could've been killed

Lisa got up to run to her front door turning to lock her door she grabbed for her phone noticing a note along
the side of her wall written in   black lipstick "I WANT THEM"…Lisa quickly called Ricky

Hello Ricky answered quickly

Ricky where are u man some girl just broke in my house and I caught the bitch

What slow down rick said calmly did u call the police? Ricky asked quickly

No Lisa answered

Why not Ricky asked

Lisa didn't want to tell him that she had the lipstick message on her wall and wanted it off first

I am about to right now

Alright I'm bout to pull up Ricky said before hanging the phone up

Lisa hung the phone up and went to the laundry room to grab some cleaning products very quickly
removing the lipstick message from her wall

Lisa dialed 911

Hello what's your emergency?

Yes I came home and someone was in my home

Ok maam what's your address and are they still there?

What a dumb question Lisa thought

No they are not after giving her the address Lisa hung the phone up to call ill babe

Lil babe didn't pick up

Lisa ran to check on the diamonds

Damn Lisa thought the bitch was close to her stash but the hoe wasn't close enough

Noticing her room window broken thinking to herself o that's how the chick got in

Wondering how would the know I got the diamonds or do she just assume

Knock knock knock

Who is it already knowing it was the police Lisa opened the door?

Hello maam we got a disturbance call from this address a tall Caucasian officer said

Yes I entered my home and it was a mess in my bedroom and someone was in here it was an women and I couldn't really see anything but I heard her voice

Maam slow down and start from the beginning

Lisa sat down noticing that she was shaken a little and slowly giving the officers the information that they needed from the beginning to end

Still in shock that number one this bitch is not running the streets and in her home and two why didn't t let her know what was going on maybe he could've informed her of this mystery women

But maybe he didn't know his self

Ok maam ok maim…the officer repeated his self

Maam are u ok? The officer asked

Lisa snapped back in huh …..I apologize … yes I understand Lisa quickly got it together with so much stuff going on she didn't want the officers to think she was going crazy

Ok just sign here and we will be on a look out and for now on make sure all of your windows and doors are locked…

Ok I sure will Lisa responded but thinking that's it? Really man

After shutting and locking the doors the officers left she could hear Ricky and James and a few other people coming to her door

O hell no all of them are not coming in here Lisa thought so Lisa hurried and grabbed her bag and shoes glasses and opened the door as if she was leaving

Hey Lisa what's up James asked

I don't know but I'm about to get a hotel for the night I don't want to be here

Ok well I'm going to be around so call if anything happen   Ricky said

Do u got your piece James asked in a low voice
Lisa just shook her head

Aright u got everything iam make sure u ok till u get to your car

Walking next to Ricky and James felt kind of awkward seeing the fact that Lisa wasn't sure of anything no more she decided to still keep it to herself about the diamonds

Well thank u guys Lisa said again before jumping in her car to head to the nearest hotel

Wondering if she should check on the diamonds before the end of the night Lisa just decided to get some rest and head to her house in the morning

Well at least that's what she was thinking… instead Lisa went to check in the hotel then straight to the nearest Walmart to get all black clothes for tonight Lisa was insisting on going by her house to check on it in the night hours

Just don't understand even before his funeral there are issues Lisa kept thinking

Lisa grabbed some cleaning spray for her tub in the hotel to scrub it

That will be 20.50 the cashier said

Lisa look down to grab her money from her purse but did not see it

Panicking Lisa turned around and didn't notice or see anyone

Excuse me miss the cashier called out to Lisa

Lisa heart started beating even faster maam cold u give me one second Lisa asked the cashier while back around   now looking at the door   Lisa seen a figure with an all-black jacket walking rather fast to the exit Lisa decided to follow as quickly as possible

Reaching for her keys that so happenily she put inside of her small denim jacket

Thank u lord they were in there still following the person in the all black jacket Lisa stopped at her car noticing the door wide open with the light on

Lisa hurried and ran to her car to see it was no one there

But her keys were along with everything that was there previously even the banana that she grabbed before leaving the hotel lobby

What is wrong with me Lisa asked herself as she walked back in the store ready to pay and leave?

I'm keeping that sir Lisa rushed to the handyman clerk that seemed to have thought Lisa was not purchasing

O I'm sorry maam the handyman clerk said

Lisa went back to the line and finally checked out

On the way back to the hotel room Lisa picked up a newspaper that was sitting on the the table in the lobby

On the front page there it was Mr. Antonio Jenkins it bring Lisa a little to her knees but ok to catch herself it was almost as if it wasn't real almost as if it was a dream

Walking into her room Lia stopped in the bathroom too spray the tub lisa was so ready to just relax and for a
Long time in her lifetime sense a time ago she got on her knees and prayed and cried and thanked the lord aboveve and asked if he could guide her into the right direction

The beds felt so great on Lisa body clean white sheets with a lot of pillows to hold and snuggle her with

Just lying there thinking like wow it all will be ok...

LISA ....Lisa ...Lisa..........scared to open her eyes because she could hear the voice of a familiar person....almost so sure she dreaming but the voice seemed so near and close before she opened her eyes she had to remember where her piece was at ...on the chaise next to her .

Lisa so scared opened up her eyes and almost shit herself

There right before her eyes stood ANTONIO

LIS u been sleep for a whole day I had to break in your house ma...like wtf...blowing your phone up and u missed your audition

Lisa blinked her eyes before jumping up and hugging tonoi so tight...tears kept coming to her eyes it was like she couldn't barely breathe...then she stopped and pinched herself to make sure it was REAL this tme

LIS baby are u ok? Tonoi asked

Yes I'm fine I just had the worst Dream in my life Lisa said...

Lisa decided to keep it to herself hell it wasn't good news news's.

Let's go eat I'm starving tonoi said let's go to somewhere NEW...

Lisa smiled and went to Get Ready!

ONE more thing came to mind so Lisa went to where she thought the diamonds were at and right there before

Lisa were the diamonds!

TO BE CONTINUED.......